FLOODS

FLOODS

PETER MURRAY

THE CHILD'S WORLD®, INC.

Photo Credits
Weather Stock: 20, 23
Comstock: cover, 2, 6, 9, 15, 16 19
Tony Stone Images/Ken Biggs: 29
Dembinsky Photo Associates/Gary Bublitz: 10, 13
Dembinsky Photo Associates/Mark E. Gibson: 30
Johnston Area Heritage Association Archive, Johnstown
Pennsylvania: 24, 26

Printed in the United States of America.

Library of Congress Cataloging-in-Publication Data
Murray, Peter, 1952 Sept. 29-
Floods / Peter Murray
p.   cm.
Includes index.
Summary: Explains how floods occur and the damage they do.
ISBN 1-56766-214-5 (hardcover : library binding)
1. Floods—Juvenile literature.   [1. Floods.]
I. Title.
GB1399,M87   1996
363.3'493—dc20   96-45346[B]
                           CIP
                           AC

TABLE OF CONTENTS

Everybody needs water. We need water to drink. We bathe in it. We cook with it. We swim in it. We water our gardens, we wash our clothes, we fill squirt guns and water balloons.

Our bodies are made mostly of water. Without water, we would crumble into dust. But what happens when there is too much water?

Rain brings water that everybody needs.

WHAT HAPPENS WHEN IT RAINS?

Every spring it rains. The water soaks into the earth. The water that the soil cannot hold runs into streams and gullies. The extra water flows into lakes and rivers. Every spring, the rivers rise. The water is held back by the banks, or sometimes spreads into the surrounding wetlands. When the rain stops, the water level slowly drops. But what happens when the rain keeps on falling?

Spring rain soaks into the earth.

In the spring of 1993, people all across the midwestern United States wondered when the rain would stop. It rained in April. It rained in May. It rained in June and in July. In Iowa, some places got three feet of rain during those months—a whole year's worth of rain in just four months!

The rivers and lakes were full, and the ground was soaked. There was no place for the water to go. It kept on raining. Every few days, there would be another downpour. Every week, the rivers rose higher.

Rain filled up lakes and rivers in the Midwest.

WHAT HAPPENS WHEN THERE'S TOO MUCH RAIN?

When there is too much rain, rivers rise above their banks and flood the surrounding land. The low-lying land on each side of a river is called a **floodplain**. When settlers first came to America, they discovered that the soil in floodplains was good for growing crops. Unfortunately, every few years the land would flood, and their crops would be washed away. Earthen banks called **levees**, and walls called **dikes**, were built to keep the rivers from flooding the land. The dikes and levees made the floodplains safe.

Or so people thought!

When there is too much rain the floodplain floods.

Nobody knew how much rain would fall in 1993. In June and July, rivers in the Midwest rose as much as fifty feet. Thousands of soldiers and volunteers spent day after day piling up sandbags to reinforce the levees. But the rain kept on falling. Billions of gallons of water spilled over the banks and levees, flooding farms and cities in nine states. The city of Des Moines was waist-deep in water. People swam through their houses, trying to save a few possessions. Farmers watched their fields turn into lakes. They had to rescue their pigs and chickens in rowboats.

And it kept on raining!

Rain spilled over the levees in Iowa.

They called it the Great Flood of 1993. Twenty-three million acres of land were flooded. Fifty people died.

By the autumn of 1993, most of the flooded land had dried out. Houses and businesses were rebuilt. Fields were replanted. Dikes and levees were repaired. But some of the floodplain was left in its natural state. The 1993 flood was especially bad because the water had no place to go. The next time the rivers rise, the floodplain will help absorb the extra water.

The Great Flood of 1993 flooded land and washed-out roads.

CAN HURRICANES CAUSE FLOODS?

People who live near the ocean sometimes get soaked by a different type of flood.

Hurricanes are gigantic, powerful storms that form far out at sea. A big hurricane can dump billions of tons of rain in minutes. Its winds can reach speeds of 200 miles per hour, causing enormous waves. When a hurricane approaches land, it pushes a huge mound of water in front of it. This gigantic wave, called a **storm surge**, can be twenty feet high. Between the rain and the storm surge, things get wet fast! Buildings, trees, people, and animals can be swept away in the rushing water.

Rain from hurricanes can cause floods.

Flooding from hurricanes has caused some of the worst disasters in history. In 1970, a hurricane struck Bangladesh, a low-lying country of lakes and rivers and streams. The sea swept over the coastal areas, killing 300,000 people. In 1991, Bangladesh was struck again, and another 125,000 people died in floods.

CAN EARTHQUAKES OR VOLCANOES CAUSE FLOODS?

Most floods are caused by too much rain. But some floods are caused by undersea earthquakes or volcanoes. When the bottom of the ocean suddenly moves, the water above it must also move. This creates a long, low wave called a **tsunami**. The tsunami moves across the ocean at speeds of up to 500 miles per hour. As the wave reaches the shallow water near shore, it rises up to tremendous heights—sometimes over 100 feet! A tsunami can occur without warning.

In 1883, a volcano on the island of Krakatoa exploded. The explosion caused a tsunami 120 feet high that killed 36,000 people on neighboring islands.

A tsunami can rise up to tremendous heights.

Sometimes floods are caused by people. In 1852, engineers built a huge dam of rocks and mud across the Little Conemaugh River in Pennsylvania. This South Fork Dam was 931 feet long and 72 feet high. Where the river was plugged by the dam, the water got deep and created Lake Conemaugh. The lake was two miles long and seventy feet deep. People used this new lake for fishing and boating. A few miles downstream, thousands of people lived in a city called Johnstown. Sometimes they joked about what would happen if the dam broke. But nobody thought it would really happen.

A dam of mud and rocks was built across the Little Conemaugh River.

The South Fork Dam held for almost forty years. But on Memorial Day in 1889, a record rainfall caused the dam to burst. A wall of water fifty feet high rushed down the valley at forty miles per hour. The people of Johnstown had no warning. The water hit the city like a monstrous wet bulldozer, ripping up houses and trees and shattering brick buildings. A railroad train was washed off its tracks. Some people escaped by floating away on the roofs of their houses. But 2,209 people died.

The Johnstown flood destroyed many buildings.

Most floods happen by accident. They are caused by unexpected rain, or storms, or earthquakes, or by a dam-builder's mistake. But the deadliest flood in modern history was caused on purpose.

In 1938, China was being invaded by Japan. The Japanese were winning. The Chinese forces were desperate. To stop the Japanese, Chinese guerrillas blew up dikes on the Huang He River. They stopped the Japanese advance, but at a terrible cost. One million Chinese people died in that flood.

Most floods are caused by storms, earthquakes, or rain.

WHY DO PEOPLE LIVE IN PLACES THAT CAN FLOOD?

Sometimes people are willing to risk floods because the land is good to them in other ways. People live near rivers because the farmland is fertile, and because the rivers are important for transportation. They say, "Next time, the levees will hold!" People live along coasts because they like to be close to the ocean. They say, "A hurricane will never strike here!" People live downstream from huge dams because they trust the engineers who built it. They say, "That dam will never break!"

And they hope that they are right!

People risk floods because the land is good to them.

GLOSSARY

dike (rhymes with "Mike")
A wall built along a river to protect land from flooding.

floodplain (FLUDD-plane)
Low-lying land along a river. After too much rain, the river sometimes spills over its banks and floods this low-lying land.

hurricane (HURR-i-kane)
A gigantic storm that develops over the ocean. If a hurricane reaches land, it can cause flooding along the coast.

levee (LEVV-ee)
An earthen bank built along a river to protect land from flooding.

storm surge (STORM-serj)
A large wave caused by a hurricane. If a storm surge hits land, it can cause terrible flooding.

tsunami (tsoo-NOMM-ee)
A long, low wave caused by an earthquake or a volcano under the ocean. Like a storm surge, a tsunami that hits the shore can cause flooding.

INDEX